THE HISTORY OF HOMEBREWING

The interaction of preparing lager has been around as workmanship for a thousand years. It's just been as of late, however, that professionals have attempted to transform it into an applied science. The most seasoned American brewery is D.G. Yuengling and Son in Pottsville, Pennsylvania, which has been preparing brew since 1829. Although we consider home preparing and fermenting of brew by and large as beginning during the 1800s, lager has been around for any longer than that. Home fermenting and lager have consistently had a large and significant influence on our lives. Truth be told, it is accepted that Noah is given to brewing to be important for the arrangements on the Ark!

What we know today as a lager was initially known as beer. The brew was made by aging the concentrate from grains and cereals. Certain spices, for example, ground ivy and stinging nettles were utilized for seasoning and bittering. Toward the beginning of the 15thCentury, individuals started to see a distinction among brew and lager, as lager was the bounced refreshment that was made in Belgium.

Lager and brew were the beverage of the everyday citizens all through the country before espresso, tea, and cocoa were presented. Religious communities were the area of a portion of the principal business distilleries in England. Numerous families, explicitly ranchers, fermented their lager (or beer), although there were proficient brewers around that made it also. Indeed, home fermenting was a family unit industry back then. The vast majority of these expert brewers comprised widows because this was one of only a handful few professional decisions open to widows. Laborers at homes frequently got brew as wages. At the point when bars appeared, they would each brew their beer. They'd put a new shrubbery outside of the spot so those passing by would know there was a new mix accessible.

In 1683, William Penn began a business of fermenting lager in Pennsburg, to bring in cash just as urge individuals to drink brew rather than hard alcohol, which appeared to caused tempers for some. The early strategies for blending brew comprised of warming and dousing grain to energize germination. The aftereffect of this blend, called malt, was then blended in with water and heated to the point of boiling until it framed the wort1, which implied it was aged. Hops2werethen added to the bubbling substance, to give it a particular fragrance and charming yet harsh taste. Bounces are utilized as a steadiness specialist and for seasoning in lager. The fluid was then stressed, at which time yeast was added. It was then permitted to mature several days. One significant distinction between preparing techniques at that point and today is the circumstance cycle. Before the 20th century, a dependable guideline or bygone era formula decided the circumstance, instead of the advanced hardware and innovation utilized today. There was a contrast between English brew and the early American lager. At the point when the English brew was made, they matured it with yeast that coasted on the top, whereas Germans utilized yeast that would remain on the lower part of the wort. At the point when the Germans eliminated the yeast, they permitted the lager to 1Wort is the unfermented or aged arrangement of malt utilized after the aged combination becomes beer2Hops come from the Humulus plant, which bears female blossoms in the shape of cones, which is the thing that is used in the blending cycle age at low temperatures for quite a long time. This brought about milder lager with a superior fragrance, making it a more mainstream style of brew.

This larger assumed control over the brewing industry, so the skimming yeast style of lager making was left for the making of beer. This was the point at which the genuine differentiation among lager and lager was made.

The late 1800's achieved numerous adjustments in the home blending of brew. It turned out to be harder for the little money manager or individual to rival the bigger distilleries utilizing around date hardware. The expansion of the railroad assisted bottling works with conveying their lager around the country. Notwithstanding, this made it a necessity that lager has the option to withstand sitting for quite a long time, temperature changes, and getting stirred up a lot of the time on the way. Synthetic added substances must be removed, and purification was important to forestall bacterial growth.

Laws happened to ensure these necessities were followed. The mid-1900s achieved the incomparable Prohibition when it was forbidden to sell any mixed refreshments. This hurt the lager and alcohol business radically, however, it endures. After Prohibition was done, it required numerous years to get individuals back prone to drink brew as opposed to hard alcohol, nonetheless. Homebrewing was made lawful in 1976 and numerous unassuming community makes brewers started making and showcasing their brands of beer, for a deal to different organizations and territories. The deals of specialty lager developed so high that they got serious to a portion of the enormous brewers, who then started creating and promoting their brands of lager.

Homemade libation isn't close just about as mainstream as it once was, with a wide range of laws that have sanctioned as the years progressed. Many have changed from the home blending of lager to take a stab at wine and different mixers. The fascinating thing about home fermenting, however, is that with every drink you make, you'll need to make a greater amount of some other assortment just to try.

PURPOSE BEHIND HOMEBREWING

Individuals decide to homemade libation for various reasons. Some appreciate the specialty of making their lager for individual utilization, while others homemade libation for the serious soul in beginner blending challenges. Others homemade libation to appropriate it at get-togethers in their home and some get it done for the leisure activity. Notwithstanding the explanation, home fermenting is still exceptionally mainstream and loads of fun once you become familiar with the craftsmanship. While the expression "home fermenting" may allude to the blending of lager, mixed refreshments and even some soda pops, it's frequently utilized while talking about the creation of brew.

In the hour of the Babylonians, lager was esteemed profoundly to the point that it was utilized as wages to be given to laborers instead of cash. Lager likewise assumed a significant part to the Egyptians, as it was fermented for sovereignty, clinical purposes and to be utilized in internments as an arrangement for the excursion to the great beyond. During the 1600s, when an Egyptian courteous fellow gave a woman a taste of his brew, it implied they were pledged. The brew was additionally utilized for installment, exchanging, giving, and burdening in the bygone eras. Thus, you can see through its type of reward today, beer was substantially more important in the past. As far back as the time 4,000 B.C., there were purposes behind home fermenting.

If you've ever gone into a bar and noticed lager consumers, you'll see that some will arrange the least expensive brew in the bar or drink whatever brand the bar ends up serving. These are false epicureans of lager. A valid and genuine lager consumer has explicit thoughts of what they need in their brew. This is another motivation behind why many pick home blending. They like a particular style of lager and flourish to get the perfect taste. Frequently there is a sure taste or style of lager that isn't accessible financially in their general vicinity, so they homemade libation to approach it out of nowhere. Home blending is, for some, advantageous as well as an approach to get the "live lager" taste. Practically all brew that is made is sanitized, so you're not getting the normal taste. At the point when lager is purified, it must be cooked, which takes out the carbonation. Business brewers "power carbonation" by taking the bubbled off liquor and blending it in with the purified lager, which murders the yeast. Without live yeast, the brew won't age-appropriately, which influences the flavor of the beer. Yeast improves the flavor of the brew, yet the tone and surface too. The more lager ages, the better it tastes, which is a huge motivation behind why so many decide to homemade libation their brew.

Another interesting use for homemade libation is a kind of fuel. Numerous ranchers that have an overflow of biomaterials, for example, rice, grains, potatoes, beets, and so on will utilize these materials to make their liquor control their homestead gear. This isn't just inventive, imaginative, and energy proficient yet also very affordable. Vehicles and trucks can likewise utilize this expense saving fuel as an option in contrast to addressing the significant expenses at the pump.

Home blending lager can be a lot less expensive than buying comparable sort lagers from business brewers, bars, or stores. Some homebrewers decide to tweak their plans as they would prefer buds, which can cost more, however, it's still generally more conservative to homemade libation their lager. Everybody appreciates an alternate taste to their lager. Also, the extraordinary taste of newly home fermented lager and the fulfillment of boasting to your companions that it's "your" brew. Jump is the substance that gives lager most of its flavor and home blending permits the creator to change the measure of bounce flavor they put in their homemade libation. Some gave brew consumers will change the measure of jump seasoning to be a lot higher than what they'd taste in a business lager. Home blending likewise offers the individual the chance to change the measure of liquor that goes into the lager since some like high liquor content though others like a milder brew flavor. Homebrewers regularly prefer to try different things with more obscure or lighter lagers and make some strength lagers that are inaccessible on the open market or exceptionally uncommon and hard to find. Besides all the evident reasons referenced here for home fermenting, it's outright and basic loads of fun. When you begin, you will not have any desire to stop. The expectation of tasting your homemade libation is something that will keep you taking a gander at the schedule. Your companions will likely all be close to home on the "testing day" when it's prepared to drink.

LEGITIMATENESS OF HOME BREWING

Many individuals that are thinking about home fermenting is worried about the lawfulness of this interaction. At the point when we consider home blending, Prohibition3comes to mind. This was a bleak period in the hearts of numerous brew consumers. It endured very long for their preferring and required numerous years to get brew back available however solid as it seemed to be preceding Prohibition. The laws have changed a ton consistently, contrastingly in numerous states and nations. Albeit home fermenting is legitimate in many regions, you should check the lawfulness in your state or country before you start this fun process. For numerous years after the Prohibition, home blending was as yet unlawful in specific territories of the United States regardless of the way that Prohibition was revoked in 1933.

In 1978, in the U.S., an Act or bill was passed in Congress for home fermenting during President Jimmy Carter's residency in office. Many individuals erroneously accept his bill permitted the home blending of brew and wine, which was around then still illicit. The bill that was passed made certain measures of home fermented brew for individual utilize excluded from tax collection. To additionally comprehend this bill and different bills for home fermenting, you can check your nearby rules.

The U.S. Constitution has given every individual express the option to direct the laws that will be basically for the assembling of home blended brew or other alcoholic substances. Try not to expect what is lawful in one state will be lawful in the following state. You would prefer not to see another leisure activity of your chance into a bad dream of legitimate issues. Alabama, for one, unmistakably expresses that it is illicit in all countries to have any gear or device used to produce any sort of mixed drinks. It's additionally unlawful there to have any illicitly produced drinks brought into the state or moved inside the state. A large portion of the states in the United States, however, do allow home preparation. There are a few limitations to the measures of lager and the age of the person brewing.

A large portion of these laws permit close to 100 gallons of homemade libation per individual per family and the individual should be over the age of 21. The maximum they can blend each year is 200 gallons. Individuals that brew their lagers are limited from selling it because the government charges liquor through extract charges. Most Western nations have similar home preparing laws. In Michigan, for example, it's entirely legitimate to blend your lager on the off chance that you are more than 21 years old however simply up to 100 gallons. You can give your homemade libation to others, however, you can't sell it. The 100 gallons, by chance, can be separated into 20 5-gallon bunches of a blend. Many home brewers like creating more modest sums all at once so they can try different things with various flavors, colors, and varieties. Kentucky, then again, restricts anybody from possessing any mechanical assembly utilized in the production of any mixed drink including homemade libation. While they are more worried about illicit refining, their laws can likewise be reached out to the home fermenting of lager.

Ensure that you don't mistake home fermenting for refining, which is very illegal in many states without specific licenses and prerequisites. Once more, your true serenity needs to check the particular laws in your region to guarantee that you will not be in lawful peril when you start this leisure activity. Laws ordinarily change from country to country or state to state. Sweden, for example, permits you to homemade libation lager as long as you don't attempt to sell it and as long as you just use it for individual use. The

United Kingdom doesn't permit people to distill or sell their homemade libation products; it's legitimate to homemade libation lager or other aged refreshments. Homebrewers don't have a cap on the amount they can make, either. Australia permits people to homemade libation their refreshments. The lone limitation is that they can't utilize a still. If any individual possesses a still, its size can't be bigger than 5 liters and it can't be utilized for the refining of liquor. The solitary use they may have for an is to in any case certain substances like water or fundamental oils.

New Zealand permits home preparing and refining starting in 1996 when the boycott against this was lifted. People can't distill spirits for their very own utilization here, however, they can't sell or supply any mixed refreshments except if they have the fitting and right permit to do so. South Africa permits people to produce aged drinks in their homes with no cutoff points on the sum.

Fascinating, however, is that they can't distill or sell their refreshments or offer them to any of their staff. The thinking behind the law for their staff is hazy except if it's a lawful issue including inebriation.

What you will discover in many states or nations is that the craft of home preparing lager, wine, or any aged drink isn't what is against the laws; rather it's the deal of these limited items. In numerous states, home preparing isn't considered in their laws since they are more worried about the production and offer of hard alcohol. Since homemade libation isn't financially fabricated and sold, it's frequently excluded from the resolutions and guidelines, leaving a ton of "ill-defined situation" in the law. Check the laws where you live before your start just to play it safe.

ADVANTAGES AND DISADVANTAGES OF HOMEBREWING

As with any pastime, there are favorable circumstances and burdens. The equivalent is valid with the home blending of brew. In any case, a great many people that decide to homemade libation their brew or different refreshments will reveal to you that the points of interest far exceed the detriments. When thinking about the main favorable position to home preparing, what rings a bell is what implies the most to brew sweethearts: taste. Drinking industrially fermented lager instead of home-prepared brew resembles eating food when you have a virus. The food simply doesn't possess a flavor like it ought to. You're not getting the full flavor. At the point when you're drinking commercially brewed brew that has been canned, packaged, presented to outside air, and thumped around, it won't taste anyplace approach as great as fresh beer. On the off chance that you don't accept this, open up a container of beer from the store, sniff it, and afterward sniff your newly fermented brew. You'll see there's no examination. All things considered, you may not have any desire to return to drinking locally acquired brew. This is presumably the primary favorable position for preparing your brew at home.

Blending your lager gives you the benefit of a solid refreshment. You might be astounded to see lager being depicted as a "solid" refreshment, however, it's sound in the perspective that you understand what's going into the brew and so forth. If you've ever taken a gander at the fixings on a container of brew or any drink besides, you'll presumably find that you don't perceive a large portion of the fixings that are going into the item. More awful than that is the way that you are devouring these new ingredients. By blending your brew, you're getting all-regular fixings that are natural to you. You're likewise not getting all the additives you get when you drink business lagers, so you're improving quality, better-tasting beer. You're acquainted with the malt, grain, bounces, or whatever other regular fixings you put in your brew. As you continued looking for great home preparing plans, you'll discover there are numerous assortments you can attempt. Despite which formula you at long last choose to stay with, you'll realize what goes in the brew. What you'll like additionally with making your brew is that you can handle the liquor content that goes in the lager.

You may like higher liquor content while your better half appreciates a milder brew. At the point when you purchase a six-pack of brew, you're compelled to drink a specific liquor content except if you need to purchase another six-pack of lower or higher liquor content. At the point when you make your blend, you can blend it up and make an assortment to suit everybody.

We should not disregard the boasting rights. At the point when you're finished making your lager, you'll likely need to host a get-together or party to flaunt your home blending abilities. It will give you a ton of pride to have the option to say that you made it yourself. Your companions will be dazzled with your culinary abilities and need to get familiar with everything they can about home preparing. Home fermented lager has a new, natural taste that you won't ever get with the monetarily prepared brew. In addition to the fact that it is a characteristic and better-tasting choice, yet additionally, it's likewise modest contrasted with what you'd pay in a store or alcohol store. The capacity to explore different avenues regarding the formula will keep on being a wellspring of good times for you. You'll never become weary of attempting various plans and making various sorts of brew. Regardless of whether it's gentle lager, high liquor substance, dim or light brew, you'll love testing until you locate the ideal mix for your new most loved formula and drink. Another bit of leeway to home preparing is that notwithstanding having a superior tasting brew, you'll likewise get it at a moderate expense. When you have all you require for your brew making adventure, you'll have the option to make lager for only a couple of pennies a lager. The least expensive sort of business brew you purchase is at any rate a dollar a container. You'll be astounded at how much lager you can brew with that equivalent dollar. As inexpensively as you can make this lager, it's a disgrace that you can't sell it!!

DISADVANTAGES

Now we'll get into the inconveniences of home fermenting your brew or refreshments. As examined before, there are not close however many drawbacks as there are preferences. Other than the wreck you'll have, one drawback to making your brew is the underlying beginning up costs. If cash and financial plan are a significant worry for you, you may think that it's hard to serenely purchase all you require to make your lager. You can ordinarily hope to put in a couple of hundred dollars to kick you off. The hardware you need will cost around $100 in addition to an enormous pot, which may cost up to $50 or more.

Remembering your store's costs for fluid and dry yeast, the whole rundown of fixings to make a 5-gallon batch can cost from $25 to $50. You'll additionally need to get some sanitizers and containers, which will cost from $10 to $20 for 24 jugs of 12-oz. size. The jugs, notwithstanding, can be reused over and over with adequate cleaning. Even though you may keep on utilizing your kitchen hardware to set aside cash, numerous individuals decide to buy exceptional gear planned explicitly for brew making. Albeit these expenses may sound costly for getting going, a large number of them are one-time costs. Also, you'll get a ton of brew for the measure of cash you've contributed. Another detriment of home preparing your brew is that you'll cherish the taste such a lot of you may end up drinking more than you utilized to and more than you ought to! Your neighbors might be over more frequently than ordinary too to get a portion of your extraordinary tasting free (at any rate to them) brew! Home fermenting can likewise be exceptionally muddled and tedious, particularly until you completely get its hang. You may choose to need an uncommon space for this cycle if you'll be doing it much of the time.

ASSORTMENTS OF HOMEBREWING

While hearing the terms, 'homebrew' makes us frequently consider lager, we are certainly not restricted to lager. Lager is generally the refreshment that the vast majority inspired by home blending start with, for the most part since it's the most well known. Another explanation is that it's the aged drink that is regularly consumed. Home fermenting of the brew is a pleasant encounter for everybody, except particularly people that appreciate a decent lager just as a variety of various flavors. You can undoubtedly change from a mellow light lager to a dull brew with high liquor content. This is the thing that most homebrewers appreciate the most about making their lager: the capacity to test until they find simply the ideal taste.

If you're a person that loves a decent glass of wine, you'll love the chance of home fermenting your wine also. For extraordinary events like parties or formal undertakings, many appreciate drinking hard alcohol. Alcohol is likewise a refreshment you'll discover fun and intrigued to make yourself. Many wine blending starter packs are accessible if fermenting wine is the thing that you need to attempt straightaway. You will not be restricted in your choice, as you'll have the option to make red wines, white wines, port ice wine, champagne, hard juice and that's just the beginning. Large numbers of the organizations that sell winemaking unit will assist you with practically any sort of wine you decide to make. You reveal to them the flavor or type you need to make and they'll help you get the correct winemaking fixing pack.

In case you're intending to make wine, later on, you might need to begin saving your old wine bottles so you will not need to put the cash in new containers. A few times the cost of the new unfilled jugs can cost nearly as much as the actual brew! Your underlying venture will incorporate the fixings and hardware, which will go around $150. A significant part of the gear that you've utilized for home blending lager can be utilized for wine and different spirits. This is particularly obvious on the off chance that you've put resources into better equipment. One thing that many homebrewers appreciate about making their wine is the kind of refreshment while they're making it. The taste is generally acceptable to such an extent that they end up drinking it while they're making it! Another sure about winemaking is that as simple as brew making is, most state making wine is considerably simpler. The normal group size you'll get with the starter winemaking packs is 6 gallons.

While that may not seem as though a great deal, it can go far. It takes the vast majority a long time to experience even one gallon of wine, substantially less six except if they drink a great deal. Most wine isn't burned-through as frequently or in such enormous amounts as beer.

A great dependable guideline with making wine is that the more extended it sits, the better it will taste. On the off chance that you find that it doesn't taste all that great, it's likely not prepared. At the point when it is prepared to drink, you'll see that it's most likely the best-tasting wine you've ever had. The blending and disinfection measure for wine just takes about 30 minutes with the packaging taking 1 to 2 hours. At that point, you stand by at least a month and a half to get extraordinary tasting wine. On the off chance that the wine was made right with appropriate sanitation techniques, it will remain new for longer than a year. The utilization of premium stops and higher liquor substance will keep it new even longer.

LIQUEURS AND CORDIALS

In a long time past, the more youthful age of consumers was generally lager consumers. While they appreciate a decent brew today, they likewise love the flavor of alcohol and cordials. On the off chance that you believe it's generally the more established age that appreciates these extravagant beverages, you were unable to be all the more off-base. Everybody appreciates a decent beverage sometimes. This is the ideal method to expand the stock in your home bar without spending an exorbitant price. The varieties of alcohol that you can make are staggering. Envision the pleasant you'll have to make Crème de Menthe, Crème de Cocoa, Irish Crème, Hazelnut, Cherry Brandy, Amaretto, Blackberry Schnapps, Peach Schnapps or Kahlua. Most homemade libation units for mixers and spirits will offer you a "base formula" in the first place and headings on the various flavorings you need to utilize. The one thing home blended alcohol shares is the taste. You'll discover no correlation between the kinds of home blended liqueur compared to financially prepared alcohol.

HOMEBREW SODA POP

While you're so bustling making your lager or alcohol, your children will wouldn't fret constantly it takes when they figure out how to make their pop. This generally basic cycle just requires about an hour or somewhere in the vicinity. You and they will love the kind of handcrafted soda, Sarsaparilla, cream pop, cherry pop, root brew, and some cola. This custom of making soft drink goes path back and is however instructive as it seems to be entertaining. Making natively constructed soft drink doesn't need a ton of gear. You'll require a siphon hose, a blending spoon, basin, a pot for bubbling, and some soft drink bottles. You'll additionally have to get a few covers and a jug capper.

Coincidentally, your children will adore utilizing the container capper and covering their jugs! These are available in any store that sells homemade libation supplies. The lone genuine fixings you'll require are seasoning packs, yeast packs, sugar, and water. Yeast packs made for refreshments works in a way that is better than bread yeast and will give your soft drink a superior taste. You'll see that making a soft drink is fun, fast and gives you and your family an extraordinary tasting refreshment.

Making your soft drink comprises of simply blending the sugar and water, adding the enhancing, blending in the yeast, and afterward siphoning it into the containers. When the jugs are full, you set the limits for them and let them sit for about fourteen days.

GLOSSARY OF HOMEBREWING TERMS

If you're new to the cycle of homemade libation, you will peruse numerous words and terms that will be new to you. While you don't have to understand what they all mean, it will be useful to have an overall thought of what the greater part of them mean. Remember that a portion of these terms might be utilized in bigger distilleries as opposed to in your home preparing measure. While there are numerous other preparing terms, these are the most widely recognized ones you will hear in your home blending.

•Additives

These substances, for example, additives, proteins, or cell reinforcements might be added to your homemade libation to add to the timeframe of realistic usability or improve the blending process.

•Adjunct

This is a fermentable material used to make a less expensive or lighter-bodied lager and subs for the customary grains.

•Alcohol

This may allude to either ethyl liquor or ethanol. At the point when the yeast works with the sugar in the malt, you get a specific liquor content, which makes it inebriating. Others portray it as the aftereffect of maturation.

•Alcohol by weight

This implies the measure of liquor that is in your brew as a level of the volume of lager. On the off chance that a container expresses its 2.5% liquor by weight, it implies it has 2.5 grams of alcohol for every 100 centimeters of beer.

•Ale

This is a kind of lager coming about because of the utilization of malted grain and the top-aging sorts of brewers yeast. Most lager you'll discover will have bounces in them, which adjust the flavor.

•All-malt

This is a brew that is produced using all-grain malt and no adjuncts.

•Alpha acids

These are the bittering compounds in jumps, which are removed when the bounces are overflowed with the wort. The higher the alpha corrosive substance, the more unpleasant the taste will be.

•Barley

This is a cereal grain, which once malted, is utilized as a crush when preparing beer.

•Barrel

This is a unit of measure used to store lager. In the U.S., a barrel is equivalent to 31.5 gallons and 36 royal gallons in Britain.

•Beer

This term alludes to the refreshments that are seasoned from bounces and contain liquor from aging grain, for example, malt.

•Body

The body portrays the thickness and property of your brew, either full or flimsy bodied.

•Bottle capper

This is a gadget used to set your crown limits for your jugs. They can be utilized for home-prepared lager or soda.

•Bottling Bucket

This container, made of food-grade plastic, has a nozzle on the base for your benefit. The preparing sugar is placed in these basins before packaging so they're at times alluded to as preparing vessels.

•Bottom-aging yeast

This is one of the two kinds of yeasts that are utilized in fermenting. Otherwise called "ale yeast", it's best when utilized at low temperatures and produces a perfect fresh taste since it matures with more sugars.

•Brew kettle

This is the vessel where the wort that comes from the pound is overflowed with the hops.

•Carbonation

This is the radiance made by the maturation and brought about via carbon dioxide.

•Carboy Brush

If you utilize a carboy, this brush is a need for cleaning. It's ideal for getting to within the carboy, which you'll need to do to clean it thoroughly.

•Conditioning tank

This is the tank where the lager is put away after the underlying maturation. This is the place where it develops and gets carbonated from the auxiliary fermentation.

•Dry-hopping

This is the point at which you add more jumps to the maturing or aging brew to build the smell or character of the bounce.

•Glass Carboy

These glass compartments, which are additionally called fermentors, are utilized to store the lager while it matures. The most widely recognized size is 5 gallons, although they arrive in an assortment of sizes.

•Hops
This is the female cone of the jumping plant, which is utilized as a steadiness and enhancing specialist in the brew and other beverages.

•Hydrometer
This instrument is utilized to quantify the heaviness of the fluid (matured or unfermented) according to the volume of water.

•Lager
This term is utilized to portray a style of beer.

•Malt
This is a grain, normally grain, which is absorbed water to get it to a specific dampness level. It at that point is sprouted and afterward cooked to be utilized in the making of lager. The measure of simmering decides how light or dull the brew will be. They are utilized as extras.

•Racking cane

This is hard plastic tubing utilized when you're moving the lager from the aging pot to the packaging basin or pot. It twists toward one side with a cap on the opposite end, which lets fluid move through with the most diminutive measure of sediment.

•Sanitizer

This is an uncommon kind of cleaner expected to purify (not simply spotless) all your hardware so it is sterile and won't advance microbes. A few people use unscented fades for this.

•Siphon hose

This hose is utilized to get the lager from the vessel or barrel into the jugs, where it will be stored.

•Sparge Bags

These sacks reused to soak the claim to fame grains or bounces in the fermenting pot. You can get reusable or expendable ones. They are soaks like teabags

•Tubing

You'll require both little tubing (3/8" or ½" inside width) and huge tubing (1" inside distance across) for your home fermenting. The little tubing is utilized to get the lager out of the fermenter and for packaging. This enormous tubing is utilized during the underlying maturation measure. Both size tubing is made of rock-solid plastic.

- Vessel

This is the compartment where the brew will be continued during the maturation period.

- Wort

This term is utilized to portray the combination of the bubbled water and malt after the bounces have been added and before it's aged.

- Wort chiller

This is utilized to rapidly cool the bubbling wort to help the yeast pitch a lot faster, which forestalls the danger of contamination. It is anything but a need, however, makes things go a lot snappier and smoother. Some decide to make their own with a tubing drinking spree and copper tubing.

- Yeast

This fixing assists with the maturation of your homemade libation. While a few people may try to utilize bread cooks yeast, brewers yeast will work much better.

EXTRAS NEEDED FOR HOME BREWING FROM SCRATCH

Now that you've perused such a great amount about home preparing, you're most likely completely energized and prepared to get moving. Even though your lager will take two or three weeks from the main day until it's prepared to drink, the real home blending measure just a few hours. Your primary concern is presumably what gear you'll have to begin home blending. A ton of this will rely upon how genuine you are about home blending. There are a couple of various variables you might need to think about.

The two primary variables are your earnestness about home preparation and your budget. If you are intense about getting into home fermenting and think you'll be doing it a ton, then you'll likely need to buy some great home blending hardware. Then again, on the off chance that you are attempting this unexpectedly and aren't sure if you'll do it once more, you're not going to need to spend a ton of cash on new home blending gear. A portion of the family unit hardware you as of now have in your kitchen may get the job done. You additionally need to remember your spending plan. If funds are a worry, you'll need to utilize what you as of now have in your kitchen or get your hardware as economically as could be expected. Large numbers of the equipment pieces recorded will make your home fermenting simpler, yet aren't a need. Something final you ought to consider when choosing what to purchase and what not to purchase is the measure of room in your home. Do you have additional room for extra gear, for example, what you'll require for home fermenting? Albeit a considerable lot of the pieces are little, some of them are bigger and will take up some space.

EQUIPMENT LIST

Here is a rundown of what you will require for brew making in your home.

- A huge pot

You'll require it to be at least 5 gallons (some utilization up to a 16-gallon size). The bigger the better because there will be less possibility for spills. This is generally a huge tempered steel pot, some of the time called your brew kettle.

- Tubing and Clamps

Clamps you can get at a store that sells home blending gear. Tubing is for the guiding of the brew. You'll need food-grade plastic tubing in both 3/8" inside measurement and 1" inside width. The huge tubing is utilized during the underlying maturation time frame and the more modest tubing is utilized to get the brew from the fermenter for bottling.

- Airtight Fermenter

You can buy a glass carboy or utilize a 5-gallon size plastic container. This is the place where you will keep your lager while it's maturing. Glass carboys come in various sizes albeit the most widely recognized size is 5 gallons. If it's in your financial plan, you'll need to go with the glass carboy since you will not need to stress over it releasing and it's extremely simple to clean on the off chance that you have an enormous brush.

•Carboy Brush

If you have put resources into a carboy, you'll need to have a carboy brush, as nothing will clean it better.

•Airlock and Stopper

There are various sizes of elastic plugs, yet you'll require 1 3/16" – 1 8/16" to fit a 5-gallon carboy. The plugs go in the opening on the carboy and the sealed areas go in the plugs. You can get a sort 1 or type 2 sealed area. The two of them work about the equivalent, yet the sort 1 is simpler to clean.

•Bottle Filler

This will be utilized when you're packaging your lager and ought to be measured so it accommodates your other tubing. This is accessible where they sell homebrew supplies.

- Thermometer

You'll require one that goes from for 32°-220° F or 0°-100°C.

- Hydrometer

This isn't a need yet is convenient. It accompanies an inspecting tube that will quantify the lager's gravity when aging. This will tell you how much sugar has been changed over to alcohol.

- Bottles

You'll need to get returnable evaluation bottles as a result of the substantial cleaning they'll require, which they are sufficiently able to withstand. In case you're fermenting 5 gallons of brew, you'll need around 60 jugs on the off chance that they're 12 oz and 32 jugs on the off chance that they're 22 oz. Try not to get the wind off cap bottles, but instead the ones where you pry off the lid.

- Bottlebrush

While this isn't a need, it will make washing your jugs much simpler.

- Bottlewasher

This appends to your spigot, goes inside the jug, and splashes water everywhere within the container, making cleaning simpler.

- Bottle caps

You'll require around 50 covers for 5 gallons of the blend, which can be bought at a homemade libation supply store.

- Bottle Capper

This convenient little gadget can be held with two hands or there's additionally one that mounts to your table and just requires one hand.

- Sterilizing solution

This is a need to keep your hardware sterile to forestall microscopic organisms and the danger of disease. A few people use unscented family unit bleach.

- Funnel

You'll require this when you pour your lager from the pot (mix pot) into the carboy.

- SpargeBag

This is utilized when you steep the claim to fame grains or jumps in the preparing pot. They come in reusable nylon or dispensable bags.

- RackingCane

This hard plastic tubing is utilized to move the lager from the fermenter to the packaging can. It has a curve on end and an exceptional cap to permit the brew to course through on the opposite end. It assists with limiting the measure of silt that streams through.

- Bottling Tube

This hard plastic cylinder has a spring-stacked tip that allows the brew to stream when it's pushed on the lower part of the lager bottle.

- Bottling Bucket

This is made of food-grade plastic and has a nozzle on the base for your benefit. The preparing sugars are placed in these before packaging, which is the reason they're now and again called preparing vessels.

- Wort Chiller

You don't must have these, yet they'll make the wort chill off significantly quicker. They come in various sizes and styles. Numerous individuals make their own with a tubing drinking spree and copper tubing.

HOME BREWING KITS

Now that you've perused the rundown of all the conceivable homemade libation supplies you may have to kick you off, you're presumably pondering where to start. Except if cash isn't a worry, you're not going to need to surge out and purchase all the new supplies recorded in Chapter 7. The sum you decide to begin with involves an individual decision. You can buy everything on the rundown, yet if you discover home preparing isn't something you will remain with, you'll have put away a ton of cash in vain. There are alternate approaches to get started with your types of gear without going through such a lot of cash. One of your alternatives is buying a home fermenting kit.

BEER MAKING KITS

You'll discover various brands of brew making kits on the market. The costs can run as low as $20 or as high as $200 and that's just the beginning. In case you're simply beginning with the home preparing interest, a home fermenting unit is going to be the least expensive option. You might not have all the provisions you'd have if you bought them all independently, however you'll have enough to kick you off. You can generally extend your stock later. A genuine famous lager making unit, The Beer Machine, can be yours for under $100 and has all you require to begin making the brew. This at-home smaller than usual distillery is made with a solid plan and development complete with a custom pressing factor check that discloses to you carbonation level, blend quality, and administering pressure. You'll have an extraordinary tasting, great lager in 7 to 10 days. Oneself controlled fermenting framework holds the normal carbonation and incorporates an assistant CO_2 carbonation framework, permitting you to have lager "on tap", exactly how you like it in public. The carbonation framework allows you to control the pressing factor utilized for administering your brew will have the ideal "head" and a new preference for as long as a half year.

Counting with The Beer Machine is the lager blend, which is blended in with water to give you 2.6 gallons of extraordinary tasting brew. You'll likewise get bar style handles, which you can customize. The Beer Machine is minimized in size so it will not occupy a lot of space on your fridge rack. This is most likely one of the least complex lager making units you'll discover and incredible for a starter kit. Other more broad brews making packs are additionally accessible. Homebrewers Outpost makes many distinctive homemade libation units. For under $100, you can get a total lager making starter unit that incorporates all the fundamental preparing hardware you'll require. With this unit, you can make 5 gallons of a brew you picked. Bit by bit bearings and plans accompany this pack alongside a large number of the provisions including maturing can, packaging pail with nozzle, hydrometer, thermometer, bottle capper, bottle covers, sanitizer, siphon unit and that's only the tip of the iceberg. The solitary thing this unit does exclude is the containers and a huge pot. On the off chance that you need to truly grow your brew making hardware stock, you can buy lager making starter units that have different embellishments like a wort chiller, choice packaging bundle, optional fermenter, luxurious kegging bundle, and additional brew making fixings.

The kegging bundle turns out extraordinary for those that don't need the object and wreck of packaging all their lager in individual containers. Along these lines, you'll generally have lager on tap, simply how you appreciate it most. These are only a few packs accessible. There are a lot more accessible available. Take as much time as is needed, glance around, and don't be hesitant to pose inquiries. Lager making packs are extraordinary because they give you all the necessities you'll require to begin, alongside headings.

It resembles an individual with no heating experience attempting to choose to purchase a total cake blend or prepare a cake without any preparation from a formula in their cookbook. Both are moderately simple, however, the cake blend will be a lot snappier, simpler, and make to a lesser degree a wreck. Lager creating units can be bought moderately inexpensively. The lone thing a few people griped about was that they at last needed to extend their stock later and that made their packs unusable for them. In case you're not going to make a great deal of brew, the packs might be your most ideal choice. In any case, on the off chance that you need to make lager routinely, you're better putting resources into the individual supplies.

From perusing the rundown of things you'll require, you may find that you now have a ton of them in your home or shop as of now, consequently saving you money.

USING THE INTERNET FOR HELP

You'll be astonished at the many site pages and lager making gatherings you'll discover on the web. You may consider buying utilized brew making gear. You can locate some extraordinary purchases on great utilized hardware that individuals at this point don't need. You certainly need to look at a portion of these spots before you make any enormous buys. Why address full cost on new gear when you can get great utilized hardware for a small portion of the cost? Beer making gatherings are an incredible spot to examine your lager making with others that appreciate a similar leisure activity. You can trade tips and learn groundbreaking thoughts while looking for a portion of the gear you may require. You'll likewise locate some extraordinary new plans from the numerous individuals here. On the off chance that you have a home blend supply store in your general vicinity, they will convey new gear, however, they may likewise have some incredible utilized hardware at a decent cost.

This is likewise a decent spot to find support or exhortation on anything you don't know about. Regardless of whether you settle on buying the gear gradually, at the same time, or going with a pack, take as much time as is needed and search for the best hardware for what you need.

INTERACTIONS OF HOMEBREWING

Now that you've mastered all you require to find out about home preparing lager, you're all prepared to begin. Home blending comprises 5 steps:

- Brewing the beer
- Cooling and Fermenting
- Priming and Bottling
- Aging
- Drinking

These headings are for 5 gallons of home-prepared lager just as essential home fermenting. You may have to roll out some slight improvements in the process contingent upon the gear you're utilizing, for example, a unit or the sort of lager you're making.

AND FINALLY...GET BREWING!

The primary thing you need to do is sanitize everything. Wash, yet additionally clean. Microorganisms may not be seen, however, they can in any case be there and ruin your whole group of brew. Homemade libation supply stores sell sanitizers or you can utilize fade. Make a blend of 5 gallons of cold water per 2 ounces of unscented bleach, utilizing your sink or a huge tub.

Clean your carboy first (if you have one), trailed by the other hardware. The things that fit in your sink can douse for 10 minutes and afterward wash them completely.

PREPARING THE WORT

Put in roughly 1/2 gallons of cold water into your enormous blending pot. On the off chance that the formula you're utilizing utilizes forte grains, put them in a sparge sack and permit them to absorb the pot and turn on the burner. At the point when it arrives at where it is practically going to bubble, take out the sparge sack. Add the malt remove into the pot and carry it to aboil once more. Allow it to bubble for 20 minutes, ensuring it doesn't bubble over. Ensure you mix the blend promptly and reliably so the malt doesn't adhere to the lower part of the container and burn.

ADDING THE HOPS

Put the necessary measure of bittering jumps in a sparge back and steep for at any rate 30 minutes. Try not to eliminate it before 30 minutes, as it needs this much an ideal opportunity for all the oils to separate from the jumps. On the off chance that your brew formula requests completing jumps (which are discretionary), placed them in another sparge sack and steep for 1 to 10 minutes. In case you're after smell, just around 2 minutes, however, if it's the flavor you're worried about, at that point 10 minutes. Turn the warmth off, take the wort off the hot burner, and put the cover on the preparing pot.

CHILL THE WORT

If you have a fermenter (glass carboy), fill it half-full with cold water. If you have a wort chiller, you can utilize this to cool the wort. If not, top off a shower of super cold (water with ice) to sit the fermenting pot in so it can chill. You may have to deplete the ice water and top it off with ice. On the off chance that you don't have a wort chiller, you'll wish you did!

PREPARING (PROOFING) THE YEAST

While your wort is chilling off, you can set up the yeast. Get a disinfected estimating cup and add 6 ounces of tepid water from the tap. Add the dried yeast to this, cover, and put in a safe spot for a piece. The warm water assists with initiating the yeast.

THE FERMENTER

If the preparing pot with the wort has cooled to where you can nearly contact it, utilize an enormous pipe to move the wort to the glass carboy (fermenter). You may utilize a little disinfected pot rather than a pipe. Fill the fermenter with cold water until you have 5 gallons (there ought to be a 5-gallon mark). For the yeast to work appropriately, it needs oxygen, which is taken out from the bubbling. To restore it with oxygen, sprinkle the water when you're pouring it in and shake the fermenter at times. Focus on the temperature, which ought to be under 75 degrees Fahrenheit. Do NOT put the yeast in the wort until the temperature is under 75 degrees or it might kick the bucket. You might need to take a perusing with your hydrometer right now to check the particular gravity.

ATTACH TUBING

Set the fermenter where it will remain cool, steady, and out of direct daylight. Get a huge solid compartment and fill it half full with water. Put it close to the fermenter. Get sanitized tubing with an outside distance across of 1 ½". Put one end in the fermenter and the opposite end in the holder of water, making a water/air proof seal. This turns into a brush off the cylinder, which will permit any excess froth to get away while the underlying maturation is occurring.

The several days, you'll truly see the yeast go to function as overabundance froth will come out the top alongside air rising out from the compartment. A few people truly love watching this interaction, realizing their lager is being made. The cylinder should remain under the water to keep the seal water/air proof. You can eliminate the pass over cylinder following 3 days and put it in the sanitized plug and airtight chamber. Ensure you add about ¾" of water to the sealed area or it will not work. You'll realize the airtight chamber is set up safely and has a decent seal if your blend begins to bubble. This is from the break of carbon dioxide.

MORE WAITING...

After you've placed it in the airtight chamber, the brew should age until the yeast is done, which generally takes from 5 to 14 days. It will be prepared for packaging when the isolated space is done gurgling. A hydrometer perusing will advise you if the maturation is finished. You're presently prepared to bottle!

BOTTLING STEPS

Once once more, you need to disinfect all that including
•bottling can,
•hose,
•bottling tube,
•racking cane,
•bottles

The containers should be completely cleaned before sanitizing them. Try not to sanitize the covers. Put them in a little pot with sufficient water to cover them. Bubble covered for five minutes, channel, and cover them again until they're required.

Add ¾ Cup of dextrose (preparing sugar) in another skillet with 16 ounces of water and bubble for 5 minutes, cover, and remove the stove.

TRANSFERRING BEER

Now you will move your brew from the fermenter to the packaging can. With the fermenter on a table, take out the airtight chamber and put in the racking stick so it's around an inch over the yeast silt. Join the packaging tube and the plastic tool to one another and fill the hose with water. Join the hose loaded up with water to the racking stick and set aside for the occasion. Put the packaging can directly underneath the fermenter on the floor and pour the bubbled dextrose in the container. Put the packaging cylinder to the base of the container and start the siphoning cycle. Attempt to sprinkle as little as conceivable as you move the beer.

BOTTLING THE BEER...FINALLY

Put the packaging basin on the table. Take the hose from the racking stick and interface it to the nozzle on the pail. You'll need to utilize a racking stick and second siphon on the off chance that you don't have a nozzle. Put a vacant jug on the floor under the packaging container. Open the nozzle and put the packaging tube in the jug, pushing down on the cylinder to get the lager going. Fill the jug right to the top. At the point when the container is full, take out the cylinder. The brew will drop down about an inch. Do this on all jugs until they're all full.

CAPPING

You require to be on a consistent surface for this, so you might need to remain on the floor. With the container capper and a cap, set a limit for the jug. Pull the switches down with a consistent pressing factor, ensuring the cap goes on straight. Crease the cap and ensure the seal is acceptable. Do this for all the bottles.

YOU'RE DONE!

All you have left to do is tidy up your wreck. Store your lager in an area with a cool and steady temperature between 65 to 70 degrees. Allow it to sit for around fourteen days and be set up to taste the best lager you've ever tasted!

RECIPES

The following are two well-known homemade libation plans that are not difficult to follow once you get the fixings. They're ideal for a 5 gallon supply. You can alter them to your very own preferences as you explore.

Grain WINE

4 to 4 ½ ounces Galena, Eroica, or Chinook bittering hops
10 to 12 pounds light malt extract
1-ounce of both Cascade and Willamette jumps (finishing)brewing yeast of your decision (many use Wyeast)

OKTOBERFEST

½-pound gem malt forte grain
6 to 7 lbs golden malt (this is an extract)
¼-lb. chocolate malt (this will be a forte grain)
½ lb. Cara-Pils Munich malt (this is a claim to fame grain)
1 ½ to 2 ounces Saaz, Hallertauer, or Tettnanger jumps (this will harsh hops)

½-ounce Saaz, Hallertauer, or Tettnanger bounces (this is your preferred completing hops)Wyeast or fermenting yeast

Some of these items may appear to be new to you, however, your homemade libation supply store should convey every one of them and then some. The plans are extremely straightforward and will make a wide range of tasting lager. When you get earnestly into the home fermenting of lager and different beverages, you'll discover there are numerous plans to be found. There's nothing more intriguing than exploring different avenues regarding various items for a one of a kind taste. Your neighborhood library will have numerous educational books on home blending just as simple-to-follow plans. The web is likewise an abundance of data with their numerous articles and lager preparing forums. There's nothing better when you take up another pastime than having the option to impart your interest to others that have similar energy. You can talk about plans you've each attempted, trade supportive clues on cash and efficient procedures you may have learned. In case you're thinking about entering novice home blending rivalries, they'll be more enjoyable on the off chance that you know a portion of the members.

THE FINISHED PRODUCT

Once you've finished making your lager, you should simply stand by out the right measure of time until you can at last taste it. Albeit each lager creator swears their homemade libation is the best they've ever tasted, it might appear to be unusual to you at the principal inspecting. All things considered, you've been drinking economically blended brew for quite a long time and this is a change. Whenever you've had a couple of your lagers, you'll never need to return to locally acquired brew again. At the point when you empty your initial brew into a glass, you'll locate a little silt on the lower part of the jug. You will not have any desire to drink this, even though it will not damage you. Your new brew will have an extraordinary taste when you open your first container. Your lager can be put away in your cooler for a long time; although it may not last all that long once everybody gets a taste.

The best time part of preparing your brew is trying different things with various fixings to build the liquor substance or give it an additional flair.

For example, numerous individuals make a home-prepared brew with maple syrup and swear it's the best they've ever constructed. Whenever you have dominated making the ideal tasting brew, you might need to explore different avenues regarding wine-making, which is the same amount of fun.

HOMEBREW FAQ

•Does it need to take this long?

While you may discover a few plans that take somewhat less time, most homemade libation needs this chance to appropriately age and age. It's more than worth the stand by.

•Do I truly need all the gear they say I need to have?

You will not need every single thing, albeit a large number of them are for your benefit. In any case, a portion of the things you as of now have in your kitchen or carport may work just fine.

•Is cleansing necessary?

Absolutely! Not exclusively can microorganisms in your lager cause a whole group to must be tossed out, however, it can likewise make you sick.

•Is home preparing safe?

Home blending is entirely protected just as being enjoyable! The possible time you may have an issue is if microorganisms discover their way into your brew. Appropriate cleansing will dispose of this problem.

•Some of my jugs detonated. Did I accomplish something incorrectly or were the containers bad?
When bottles detonate, they were filled excessively high or there was a lot of dextrose (sugar) put in your brew. The contains ought to be filled just mostly the neck. On the off chance that you didn't stand by the necessary time before packaging the brew, the sugar might not have had the opportunity to separate the liquor, which may make them explode.

•Why does my lager have a severe taste?
Everyone has distinctive taste buds, however, you may attempt to place fewer bounces in your brew next time you make it.

•Should I use malt concentrate or claim to fame grains when I make my beer?
Using grains is somewhat more convoluted than utilizing malt extricates. Malt separate is a powder or syrup that is produced using grains. In case you're a novice at making your lager, you're in an ideal situation remaining with malt separate until you truly get the hang of exploring different avenues regarding home blending. The absolute best brews on the planet are made with malt extricate.

•This is my first time making my lager. I've perused all that I can to gain proficiency with the cycle. I need to take a stab at making lager, yet I would prefer not to go through a ton of cash simply beginning. Should I purchase all the necessary hardware or simply purchase the kit?

Although having all the necessary gear will be advantageous for you in the future, all the things may appear to be overpowering unexpectedly home the brewer. You might need to buy the pack for your first brew making experience. The benefit of utilizing a homemade libation unit is that there are fewer things to stress over, you have all you require and there are not difficult to follow bearings. What many appreciate about the units is that the plans they incorporate depend on their packs, so you don't need to change any bearings.

•How do I realize the best spot to purchase my provisions and equipment?

Once you have made your first bunch of lager, you'll discover somewhat more about what it involves and what you need. Shop around in your neighborhood well as on the web. The most ideal approach to get the best hardware for your cash is to explore what you need and locate the best cost.

www.ingramcontent.com/pod-product-compliance
Lightning Source LLC
Chambersburg PA
CBHW081158130726
47996CB00009B/3170